A First Welsh Country Cakes and Buns

traditional
tea-time favourites
from the country kitchens
of Wales
by
Bobby Freeman

y Lolfa

TEA-TIME in Wales is a delight, for the Welsh are very fond of all kinds of cakes and buns and all the delicious batter scones and pancakes traditionally made on the bakestone (griddle) – and this is where much of the old cookery of Wales is still very much alive and well.

In rural Wales, freshly-baked sponges and fruit cakes and the ubiquitous Welsh cakes appear like magic however unexpectedly you call at tea-time. On goes the kettle and out come the pretty flowered china cups with gold about their rims that grace every country tea table – and most town ones as well. Woe betide you if you do not do justice to the spread!

So numerous are the Welsh tea-time recipes that it has taken three of these little books to deal with them all. There are so many good and often unusual recipes, plus some deceptively simple ones which turn out to be scrumptious – especially if they are made as they should be, in the old way with brown sugar and butter. This is one way of telling an old recipe from a more recent version which will usually say 'margarine' and just 'sugar', meaning white sugar. Of course times have changed and there are now margarines and margarines, and proper unrefined brown sugar has the health argument going for it, but this is no place for me to get into the health argument — the choice is yours.

But with such a wealth of choice, I think it is a pity that more has not been made of tea-time in Wales for tourists. It's more than likely that when the English began to invade Wales as holidaymakers, the Welsh with their innate sense of hospitality tried to offer the visitors what they were accustomed to — to English tea — and so Welsh tea-time delights remained hidden. Even now, with tourism well developed and highly organised by a national tourist board, a real Welsh tea is hard to find outside Welsh home.

Here then is a selection of the cakes and buns traditonal to Wales — some associated with the farming year — like shearing and harvest-cakes devised to feed a hungry host of helpers, for Wales was a country of small farmers who helped each other at such times (and still do, despite change). Some are connected with the mines and quarries — lunchtin cakes, some with old fairs and religious feast days. There are some very old recipes here, too — one from a MS cookery book of the early 18th century, and three from the diary of an 18th century Gwent farmer's wife.

And one from the Welsh settlement in Patagonia, where, after the successful damming of the river Camwy, overplus of dairy produce created rich recipes far removed from the frugality of the life the emigrants had left behind in Wales.

3

Souly Cakes
Cacennau Enaid

These were a Gower speciality, a yeast bun mixture shaped as a person like a gingerbread man: 'brown, spiced and shiny, with a round head, currant eyes, semi-circular smile, made on All Soul's Day, the Christian version of the pagan feast of that day' according to a local description. They were similar to the 'pop' dollies of the traditional west-country fare and almost certainly the idea was imported from Devon and Somerset via the cross-channel trade which markedly influenced the customs, speech and food of the glorious little peninsular so amazingly occurring between industrial Llanelli and Swansea.

On Gower they kept the 'old style' day as in the Welsh year (New Year's Day January 13th) on November 12th, not the 2nd as in the Christian year. On 'Souling Day' the

1 lb plain flour (pref. strong flour)
1 oz yeast
3 ozs sugar
2 ozs butter
2 ozs currants or sultanas
pinch salt
1 egg
milk to mix
METRIC: 450g flour; 25g yeast; 75g sugar; 50g butter; 50g dried fruit

4

children of Gower would call round the houses asking for cakes with this old souling song:

> 'Souly, Souly, Christendom,
> Every good woman give me some,
> Give me some or give me none,
> Give me an answer that I may be gone'.

Warm the flour. Set the yeast to froth in a little of the warmed milk. Rub the butter into the flour, add the sugar and salt, make a well in the centre and pour in the frothed yeast with the egg beaten into it, with sufficient warm milk to make a soft dough. Knead well, add the dried fruit and leave to prove in a warm place under a cloth or polythene for 1-2 hours, or until doubled in size. Knock back, shape into 'men', using currants for the eyes, etc, leave to rise until doubled in size again, set well apart on a well-greased baking tin (about 1 hour). Bake in a hot oven (400°F, Gas 6, 200°C) for 15-20 mins. Brush immediately with honey or sugar glaze (2 tbls. sugar or honey boiled with the same of milk until syrupy), and again when the first coat is dry.

Llanddarog Fair Cakes

Teisennau Llanddarog

Llanddarog is a village in Dyfed, in contemporary terms
on the main Swansea—Carmarthen road. More
significantly, and to explain these cakes, it lay on one of
the old drovers' routes. They were made with beer, which
helped to keep them in good condition for a long while,
thus they were popular with the drovers for their long
journeys to the English grazing lands. They were about 6
in long, 3 in wide, ¼ in thick, and cost 2d each.

12 ozs SR flour
8 ozs butter
6 ozs sugar
¾ tablespoons beer
currants
METRIC: 350g flour; 225g·butter; 175g sugar

Mix flour and sugar together and rub in the butter. Make
a stiff dough with the beer, roll out to ¼ in thick and cut
into rectangles. Use currants to mark like dominoes. Bake
in a moderate oven for 20-30 mins until golden. Makes
about 24.

James' Cakes
Cacennau Iago

These little shortbread cakes, marked with a scallop shell, were made at Aberffrau, a fishing village on the west coast of Anglesey where the shells were found on the beach. They are nearly always called Aberffrau or 'Berffro' cakes, appearing under the former in 'Cassell's Dictionary of Cookery', 1885. But they are more properly called after St James—pilgrims *en route* for the church of Santiago de Compostela in Spain's north-western province of Galicia wore a scallop shell as a hat badge. Note that the two Celtic countries, Wales and Galicia, share the name for James.

3 ozs flour
2 ozs butter (softened)
1 oz sugar
METRIC: 75g flour; 50g butter; 25g sugar

Beat the sugar into the softened butter, then add the flour a little at a time, with your hands. Work the dough on a floured board, then roll out and stamp into rounds with a plain cutter, keeping them as thin as possible. Mark each round with a scallop shell (I have one from Aberffrau) and trim to a shell shape if liked. Bake quickly in a hot oven (425°F 218°C, Gas 7) on a greased baking sheet.

They should not turn brown and need watching carefully. Sprinkle with sugar while still warm.

Moist Cake
Teisen Lap

The early version of this enduringly popular Welsh cake
was a 'batter cake', made with sour cream and baked in a
Dutch oven before the fire until it was nice and scrunchy,
as one Welsh friend told me. Often it was made as a
means of using up cream when there wasn't enough for a
churning of butter. As most Welsh recipe collections give
the later, basic fruit cake recipe, I'm giving the early one,
which is well worth trying. Instead of a Dutch oven you
can use a grill or a low oven.

The 'cake' version was usually baked on an enamel plate
as *teisen blat* (plate cake). Because of its moistness it was
popular with miners for their 'snaptin' containing their
mid-day meal. Someone in North Wales suggested that
teisen lap developed into the commercial bakers' slab cake.

1 pint sour cream
3 ozs butter
4 ozs sugar
4 ozs sultanas
1 egg
3 ozs self-raising flour
METRIC: 575ml (20 fl. ozs) cream; 75g butter; 125g sugar; 125g sultanas; 75g sugar; 75g flour

Rub the butter into the flour, add the sugar and sultanas,
beat the egg into the cream and mix thoroughly. Pour into
a shallow tin and bake in a low oven (250°F, Gas ½,
130°C) or in a low position under a hot grill.

Ann Davies' Cake
Cacen Ann Dafis

Ann Davies was a baker in Kidwelly in south-west Wales at the beginning of this century, famous for her fruit cake which she sold from the shop in front of her bakery at 6d a pound (2½p). She was apparently prepared to part with her recipe, probably for a small sum, as bakers then did sometimes sell their recipes. This one was much prized by housewives in south Wales.

1½ lbs plain flour
1½ lbs currants
1 lb sugar
¼ lb butter, ½ lb lard
½ pint milk, 2 beaten eggs
½ teas. each nutmeg, mixed spice
½ teas. baking powder, ¼ teas. salt
METRIC: 675g flour; 675g currants; 450g sugar; 125g butter; 225g lard; 275ml (10fl. ozs) milk

Sift all the dry ingredients together (except the currants) then rub in the butter. Add the currants. Make a well in the centre, pour in the eggs and mix together, gradually adding the milk, until you have a fairly soft consistency. Grease two cake tins, divide the mixture equally between them and bake in a moderate oven (350°F, Gas 4, 180°C) for about 1½ hours.

Shearing Cake
Cacen Gneifo

Sheep-shearing time was, and still is, one of the major
social occasions in Welsh rural life, for in the difficult hill
districts especially farmers help each other with the
rounding-up and shearing of their enormous flocks of
sheep on a rota basis. The host farm kitchen is busy for
days beforehand preparing pies and tarts and cakes and
baked meats ready to feed the shearers. This cake, with its
caraway seed flavour, is traditional to shearing-time:

8 ozs flour
6 ozs moist brown sugar
4 ozs butter
¼ pint milk
1 egg
1 teas. baking powder
2 teas. caraway seeds
rind of ½ a lemon
a little grated nutmeg
METRIC: 225g flour; 175g sugar; 125g butter; 150ml (5fl. ozs) milk

Sift the baking powder with the flour, mix in the other dry
ingredients. Rub in the butter, then work in the beaten egg
and milk. Bake in a greased tin lined with greased paper in
a moderate oven (350°F, Gas 4, 180°C) for 1 hour.

Threshing Cake
Cacen Ddyrnu

Like harvest and sheep-shearing, threshing time was an occasion for feeding a hungry number of workers, and this is the cake traditionally made for it . . . and for shearing-time too. Note the use of bacon dripping, often used in cake-making in Wales in the old days, for there was always plenty of it with bacon the most usual meat. You can of course substitute lard or vegetable fat if you wish, but the bacon fat does impart a distinctive flavour to the cake.

1 lb plain flour
1 lb mixed currants and raisins
8 ozs sugar
8 ozs bacon dripping
2-3 eggs, well beaten
1 teas. bicarb. soda
buttermilk to mix
METRIC: 450g flour; 450g dried fruit; 225 sugar; 225g bacon fat

Dissolve the bicarb. soda in a little tepid water mixed with some of the buttermilk. Add the beaten eggs with the bicarb. soda mixture and enough buttermilk to the flour to give a fairly soft consistency. Bake in a greased cake tin in a fairly hot oven (400°F, Gas 6, 200°C) for about 1½ hours.

Spice Cakes

Potato Cake
Poten Dato

This was a favourite with children. In the potato-growing counties of the west—Pembrokeshire and Cardiganshire—it was a cheap and ready stand-by, often made in a big tin in the bread oven after the bread had been taken out, as were other cakes and puddings. Older folk still speak of it with fondness, and indeed it is nice.

1 lb (approx.) (METRIC 450g) boiled potatoes
1 egg, well beaten
plain flour
sugar
spice
currants
milk
butter
salt—all these are variable to taste

Mash the potatoes with a few lumps of butter in a bowl. Work in the dry ingredients, then mix in the egg and milk to give a fairly soft consistency. Bake in a greased, shallow tin in a moderate oven (350°F, Gas 4, 180°C).

Honey & Ginger Cake
Teisen mel a sinsir

A rich, old cake from the times before cheap sugar became available, with dried fruits as well as honey contributing to the sweetness, and no sugar at all. Honey is also a moisturiser so this cake can be kept for about a fortnight in an airtight tin.

1 lb plain flour
4 ozs butter
2 eggs
3 ozs sultanas
3 ozs glace cherries (halved)
½ lb runny honey
2 large teas. baking powder
2 large teas. ground ginger
a little candied peel
pinch of salt; milk to mix
METRIC: 450g flour; 125g butter; 75g sultanas; 75g cherries; 225g honey

Melt the butter over a low heat, dissolve the honey into it together with a little milk. Leave to cool. Sift the flour, salt, baking powder and ginger together, then add the sultanas, peel and cherries. Add the beaten eggs to the honey and butter and then to the dry mixture. Mix thoroughly, using a little more milk if necessary. Bake in a greased baking tin in a moderate oven (350°F, Gas 4, 180°C) for 1-1½ hours.

Cinnamon Cake
Teisen Sinamon

An impressive cake, its dark base contrasting with a deep meringue topping, is created by the simple improvement on the original of just one extra egg yolk, and one, or perhaps two, egg whites.
It was such a success in my former restaurant that I was continually asked for the recipe.

8 ozs flour
4 ozs sugar
4 ozs butter
2 egg yolks, 2-3 egg whites
½ teas. baking powder, 1 teas. cinnamon
jam; milk to mix
METRIC: 225g flour; 125g each sugar and butter

Sieve the flour and baking powder and rub in the butter. Add the spice and sugar, then the egg yolks and a little milk to bind to a fairly stiff sponge. Turn into a shallow, well-greased tin or plate—preferably a dish you can serve it in as the base is best left where it is. Bake in a hot oven (400°F, Gas 6, 200°C) for about 20 mins. Cool and spread with jam—apricot or raspberry.

For the meringue topping, beat the egg whites until stiff, fold in 1 tbls. caster sugar for each white and beat again in the usual way until shiny. Pile on top of the base and return to a cooler oven (325°F, Gas 3, 170°C) to set and until the peaks are tipped with gold.

Ginger Cake without Ginger
Teisen sinsir heb sinsir

Was the ginger left out of this recipe just because it was forgotten—or because it was so obvious an ingredient? Or is it meant to represent ginger cake without actually having any of the spice? Because it does have a gingery taste. I found the recipe first as 'Old Welsh Gingerbread' with the information that it used to be sold at the old Welsh fairs.

8 ozs flour
4 ozs butter
6 ozs black treacle
6 ozs brown sugar
½ teas. bicarb. soda
1 teas. cream of tartar
2 ozs chopped mixed peel
¼ pint milk
METRIC: 225g flour; 125g butter; 175g treacle; 175g sugar; 50g peel

Warm treacle slightly and mix in the milk. Sift the dry ingredients together and rub in the butter. Add sugar and peel, stir in treacle and milk. Bake in a greased tin for 1½ hours at 350°F, Gas 4, 180°C.

Gingerbread
Mrs. Griffiths Jones'
manner

from the MS cookery book compiled by Anne Phelps at
Withybush House (Poyston East), Haverfordwest
(Pembrokeshire Record Office).

An early, and very good mixture for ginger *biscuits*,
with all the spices included to indicate its authenticity
as the genuine British gingerbread. Simply reduce the
quantities by about a third.

'Take three pounds of flour, two pounds of Butter
without salt, two pounds and a half of Treacle; rub
into the flour one pound of brown sugar, with one
ounce of grated Ginger, a large Nutmeg, and half an
ounce of Caraway seeds either ground, or beaten; melt
the butter and work the above articles with it adding as
much Pearl ashes (bicarbonate of soda) as will lie upon
a shilling—pour into the Treacle a glass of Brandy or
Rum and mix the whole well together; drop it with a
spoon upon tins buttered and floured, take care the
Oven is not too hot to burn them.'

OVEN TEMPERATURES

Slow	240° – 310°F	115° – 155°C	¼ – 2
Moderate	320° – 370°F	160° – 190°C	3 – 4
Fairly Hot	380° – 400°F	195° – 205°C	5
Hot	410° – 440°F	210° – 230°C	6 – 7
Very Hot	450° – 480°F	235° – 250°C	8 – 9

"The Cottager's Stove,"
WHICH REQUIRES NO BRICKWORK TO FIX IT.

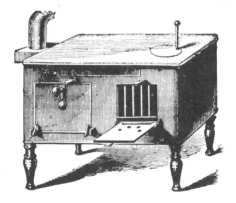

Fruit Cakes

Patagonia Black Cake
Cacen Ddu Patagonia

At first glance, this appears to be just another rich dark fruit cake, until one comes to the final stage of embalming it within a crisp casing of thin icing, when it begins to bear some resemblance to the Black Bun of Scotland. What gives it its association with South America is the rum, nicely entrapped within the cake's innermost recesses—the result is a cake which can be made well ahead of times of

10 ozs butter
10 ozs dark brown sugar
4 ozs each raisins, currants, sultanas
8 ozs mixed peel
4 ozs chopped nuts (walnuts or almonds)
1 lb plain flour
4 eggs
1 teas. each cinnamon and mixed spice
2 teas. baking powder
1 teas. almond essence
1 teas. bicarb. soda mixed in 1 tbls. vinegar and 1 tbls. water
a small glass of rum
METRIC: 275g each butter and sugar; 450g flour; 125g each raisins, currants, sultanas, nuts; 225g mixed peel

celebration and kept, in cool conditions, maturing for months.

A recipe from the descendants of the Welsh emigrants who settled in Patagonia in the mid 18th century.

Grease and line an 8in cake tin. Cream the butter and sugar, adding the lightly whisked eggs a little at a time, beating well. Fold in the sieved flour and spices, the dried fruit and nuts. Pour the liquid with the two raising agents, together with the almond essence, on to the mixture and mix thoroughly. Lastly add the rum.

Bake on the middle shelf of a moderate oven (325°F, Gas 3, 170°C) for 3-3½ hours.

For the casing;

6 ozs icing sugar (METRIC: 175g)
3 tbls. hot water, mixed as a thin, glace type icing.

Brush all over the cake—top, sides and bottom—to completely encase it in a brittle sugar shell. This is easier to do while the cake is still warm.

Boiled Cake
Teisen Ferw

When I was given this recipe by a Swansea woman many years ago, it was quite unfamiliar to me. I therefore accepted the instruction to boil the fruit, sugar and butter together for 2-3 *hours* . . . although I thought it a little odd! Of course it should have read minutes, not hours. But I did in fact try the recipe out as it stood, simmering the mix for all of two hours. It has to be said that the result was a lovely, dark, rich cake.

Like *teisen lap* this cake was a useful portable for meals eaten at the workplace. The first stage is to simmer together) for a few minutes (or 2 hours):

12 ozs mixed dried fruit
8 ozs butter
8 ozs soft brown sugar
½ pint milk
METRIC: 350g dried fruit; 225g each butter and sugar; 275ml (10fl. ozs) milk

Leave to cool for 15 mins, then add:

1 lb plain flour (metric 450g)
1 teas. mixed spice
1 teas. bicarb. soda
1 teas. salt
2 eggs

Mix well. Turn into a greased cake tin and bake in a moderate oven (350°F, Gas 4, 180°C) for 1-1½ hours.

Other . . .

Shortbread
Bara Brau

This recipe will please wholefood enthusiasts as it is traditionally made with wholewheat flour. It would be made for special occasions such as the *nosen lawen* (merry evenings) which were such a feature of Welsh rural life in the past. They were neighbourhood gatherings for song, dance, story and harp music, usually in the hospitable kitchen of the largest farmhouse, in which everyone contributed a 'turn'. Today, the delightful *'Hwyrnos'* at Plas Glansevin at Llangadog near Llandeilo in Carmarthenshire (Dyfed) gives an impression of the *nosen lawen* atmosphere.

6 ozs butter
10 ozs wholewheat flour
3 ozs rice flour
6 ozs caster sugar
METRIC: 175g butter; 275g flour; 75g rice flour; 175g sugar

Soften the butter and work into the flours and sugar until you have a soft dough. This is a job for warm hands. Shape into one or two flat rounds on shallow baking tins, well greased. Prick the surface with a fork and thumb-pinch the edges in the traditional shortbread fashion. Bake in a moderately hot oven (375°F, Gas 5, 190°C) for about 30 mins.

Gwent Hazelnut Sandwich

Teisen Cnau Cyll Gwent

On a farm near Chepstow in 1796, Anne Hughes, the farmer's wife, wrote a diary of the year's day-to-day events of which she was the loving, practical hub. The diary includes many recipes, all imprecise in our present-day terms but capable of interpretation.

Attributed to Cousin Floe, this rich hazelnut sponge recipe was intended to be cut up 'in divers shapes', but to my mind it is better left whole. The toasted hazelnuts are what make the cake special.

5 ozs SR flour
4 ozs caster sugar
4 ozs butter or soft margarine
3 eggs
3 ozs finely chopped hazelnuts
METRIC: 125g flour; 125g sugar; 225g butter; 75g nuts

Beat the butter and sugar together until creamy, add eggs and flour alternately. 'Then she did take two shallow tins and poured the mess in equal lots and bake in the oven 30 mins of the clock' (375°F, Gas 5, 190°C). 'Before she did bake them she did chop up sum filber nuts and sow over the top of both cakes'. Anne Hughes used butter cream and jam to sandwich the sponges together (nuts uppermost on the top half) but jam beaten into whipped cream is nicer, I think.

Apple Cake
Teisen Fala

This is unexpectedly delicious, especially when eaten
warm with lots of cream. The mixture can also be divided
into a bun tray to make what the English call 'apple
muffins'.

10 ozs SR flour
5 ozs butter
5 ozs brown sugar
1 lb cooking apples
milk to mix
METRIC: 275g flour; 150g each butter & sugar; 450g apples

Rub the fat into the flour, add the sugar. Peel and core the
apples and cut into tiny dice. Mix all together with a little
milk to bind to a fairly stiff dough. Spread into a well-
greased shallow tin and bake for about 30 mins. in a
moderate oven (350°F, Gas 4, 180°C).

Honey Dough Cake
(from Anne Hughes' Diary)

Make this on bread-making day, as Anne Hughes did:

'I do take a peese off the bred doe and maken a hole in the middle, I do put in some furme (firm) honey. Then I do neede and patte it, taking care to keep the honey inside. Then I do poke in sum swete plums (raisins) inside as well as out, then pat it flat aboute a finger thick, and bake it in the oven. When done it be all browne and swete on the top, and makes good etting.'

Elevenes Cake
Teisen Te Deg

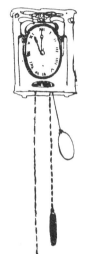

A good, plain standby cake from Ceredigion, quickly made and baked, and useful as its name suggests for the mid-morning break.

8 ozs plain flour
½ teas. bicarb. of soda
4 ozs butter or margarine
3 ozs sugar
1 egg
pinch salt
milk to mix
METRIC: 225g flour; 125g butter; 75g sugar

Sift the dry ingredients. Cream the butter and sugar and gradually add the flour alternately with the beaten egg and enough milk to give a soft, dropping consistency. Bake in a greased tin in a moderate oven for about 1 hour (350°F, Gas 4, 180°C).

Seed Cake
Teisen Carawe

The oldest and most enduring of our sponge cakes, caraway seeds offering no obstacle as early cooks experimented with the newly-discovered raising power of eggs. It's still liked by older people in Wales today, for whom it must be inextricably linked with memories of chapel and Sunday tea in the front parlour with everyone on their best behaviour.

1 lb plain flour
8 ozs butter
5 ozs caster sugar
2 teas. baking powder
2 eggs
½ oz caraway seeds
METRIC: 450g flour; 225g butter; 200g sugar; 10g caraway seeds

Sieve flour and baking powder. Rub in the butter. Add the sugar. Beat the eggs with a little water and mix all together—a fairly stiff mixture. Bake 1-1½ hours in a moderate oven (350°F, Gas 4, 180°C).

Rollies
(from Anne Hughes' Diary)

'. . . which be made by putting sum flour in a bowl then drop in 4 eggs and a bit of sugar and beet it up to a soft mess, then put in a long tin and bake gentlie. When it be cooked, I do turn it out gently on a board and put on sum swete plums and nut-meg and sprinkel with sugar, then roll it up and put away till cold.'

3½ ozs SR flour
3½ ozs caster sugar
4 eggs
METRIC: 110g flour; 110g sugar

Whip the eggs and sugar with a loop, rotary or electric whisk until light and foamy, then lightly fold in the flour. Level off in an oiled oblong sponge tin and bake at 350°F, Gas 4, 180°C for about 25 mins, when the centre should be springy to the touch. Turn out and cool on a wire rack and treat as Anne Hughes suggests—'swete plums' are large raisins.

Buttermilk Cake
Cacen Llaeth Enwyn

Another Ceredigion recipe—interesting to try if you can get fresh buttermilk, which is increasingly becoming available in rural areas at least.

8 ozs flour
½ teas. baking powder
4 ozs butter
4 ozs brown sugar
8 ozs mixed dried fruit and a little candied peel
¼ pint buttermilk
METRIC: 225g flour; 125g butter, 125g sugar; 150mls (5fl ozs) buttermilk; 225g fruit

Sift the flour and baking powder and rub in the butter. Add the dried fruit. Mix to a fairly stiff consistency with the buttermilk and bake in a lined cake tin in a moderate oven (350°F, Gas 4, 180°C) for about 1 hour.

In this series

1. A Book of Welsh Bread
2. A Book of Welsh Country Cakes and Buns
3. A Book of Welsh Bakestone Cookery
4. A Book of Welsh Country Puddings and Pies
5. A Book of Welsh Fish
6. A Book of Welsh Soups and Savouries

Also by Bobby Freeman

Lloyd George's Favourite Dishes (1974, 1976, 1978—Ed.)
Gwent—A Guide to South East Wales (1980)
First Catch Your Peacock—A Book of Welsh Food (1980)
Welsh Country House Cookery (1983)
Welsh Country Cookery—Traditional Recipes from the Country Kitchens of Wales (Y Lolfa, 1987)

First impression: 1984
Reprinted (Y Lolfa): 1987
Reprinted (Y Lolfa): 1993
Reprinted (Y Lolfa): 1994

ISBN 0 86243 138 7

Printed and published in Wales by
Y Lolfa Cyf., Talybont, Dyfed SY24 5HE;
Phone: 0970 832 304, fax: 0970 832 782.

Please send for our free 80-page catalogue!